P9-DWW-269

CALGARY PUBLIC LIBRARY

DEC   2016

IN THIS PLACE

IN THIS PLACE

CALGARY 2004 – 2011

PHOTOGRAPHS BY GEORGE WEBBER
WORDS BY ARITHA VAN HERK

George Webber

Aritha van Herk

fhm Frontenac House Media Ltd.

Published by
Frontenac House Media Ltd.
Building B1, Suite 136
2451 Dieppe Ave. SW
Calgary, Alberta T3E 7K1

Photographs copyright © 2011 by George Webber
Text copyright © 2011 by Aritha van Herk

Printed and bound in Canada

Library and Archives Canada Cataloguing in Publication

Webber, George, 1952-
      In this place : Calgary 2007-2009 / photographs by George
Webber ; text by Aritha van Herk.

ISBN 978-1-897181-59-1

      1. Calgary (Alta.)--Pictorial works. 2. Calgary (Alta.)--History--
21st century. I. Van Herk, Aritha, 1954- II. Title.

FC3697.37.W42 2011   971.23'38040222   C2011-906450-2

Book and jacket design: Epix Design Inc.

All rights reserved, including moral rights. No part of this publication may be reproduced or transmitted
in any form or by any means, electronic, mechanical, photocopying, recording, or otherwise, or placed
in any information storage retrieval system without permission in writing from the author or publisher, or
a licence from The Canadian Copyright Licensing Agency (Access Copyright), except by a reviewer or
academic who may quote brief passages in a review or critical study.

Frontenac House Media gratefully acknowledges the support of the Canada Council for the Arts for our
publishing program. We would also like to thank the Government of Alberta Multimedia Development
Fund for their support of our publishing program.

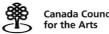

Canada Council   Conseil des Arts
for the Arts   du Canada

**Government
of Alberta** ■

DEDICATIONS

Dedicated to my sisters' children: Ben, Ty, Trish and Beth Baines; Joseph, George, Thomas and William Lace; and Joel and Nicole Michaud, who give me good reason to believe in the future.

    – George Webber

This book is for my Calgary friends, loving and supportive, happy companions.

And to the memory of Bob Edwards, *Eye Opener* critic of Calgary, an irascible voice that still models how to be outspoken without snark, generous without flattery.

    – Aritha van Herk

IN THIS PLACE

WORDS BY ARITHA VAN HERK

FENCES

Trace their double helix back to barbed wire, Calgary's connective fences. How they propose a puzzle. The First Peoples had never seen such a constrict. What kind of idea is that? Designed to stop movement, to herd what it encloses, to possess. As if this world could be coralled, could be divided.

The fence: demarcation or inclusion, meant to score undulating land into tractable wedges. A fence tries to harvest space, refusing the very impossibility of what it cannot surround.

Fences were born from humans writing over earth, signatures scrawled across the face of fescue and prairie wool. They interrupted herds of antelope, the last few buffalo stumbling into barbed wire and shaking their shaggy heads in puzzlement.

How do you grow a fence? Claim and resistance, stake out the prairie's delicate bones, perimeter its rough, expose a skeleton as if it were a specimen.

There is an ecology of fences. They are determined to disappear disappearance, to divide and conquer. They declare an edge, a selvage, a property line, all the while displaying mordant wit. They will dance themselves to death, torture their own restraint. They speak the cryptic language of containment and exclusion, wordless and fragmented, earthbound.

And yet, urban fences are indelible as ghosts, idiomatic as speech. Worming between streets or standing shyly back from sidewalks, they possess their own corroded charm, homesick as any separation, prelude to privacy's secret diversions.

Chain link and leaning, sprawled around rough patches of industrial refuse, they are human traces marking work and property. No elegant fittings, no fancy Victorian wrought iron topped with *fleur de lis*, but tough and galvanized, and like this city, on its feet. Three strands of barbed wire necklacing the top. "Danger: Keep out."

Our fences do a job, rough diamonds knitting together patches of air. They wear steel-toed boots, they do not decorate but flex, they measure force and displacement. They are sweaty after a couple of years, rusty past decades, sagging and forlorn in old age. They frame views and tranquility, navigate boundaries of energy that wax and wane with the properties they measure.

Our fences smuggle what they are supposed to hide, offer alternative crossings, ways to ride lines. They invite delicious trespass, seduce the eye into viewing the other side. No liability, or consent, just the heady sense of pushing through a hole in a fence, not having to go around or re-direct. A fence is an invitation to resist, a calculus of invasion, sweet with transition.

Calgary's fences scout the landscape, ride it like rattler lines, come up against thunder, muffler roar and the treacle of asphalt. They are nets holding the streets together, breathless labyrinths that feign disdain. These fences are clumsy with affection. They attach themselves like playground friends. They look back at us patrolling their circumference, stare past horizons of discovery with a shy invitation to regard the unseen, that which they cannot conceal. Calgary's fences oxidize patience. Tarnished, discoloured, they rust beside us, dozing past back alleys and around vacant corner lots.

Only the blue range of the sky measures out the cross and pattern of containment, fracturing blocks and yards into chunks. Fencing's genetic linkage, Calgary's optimistic chromosomes, lattice resistance. Open range is never open.

And yes, our fences can alienate one patch of grass from another, can render joyless railway tracks and auto body yards. Steel fittings and aluminum wire speak a plain language, economical and pragmatic. Hoardings propose a future, surely better than the muddy construction site within. And every fence can be festooned by signage, as if the air it proposes to enclose dare not go to waste.

Celebrate the missing teeth of the white picket, remnant of the 50s. Toast the fence leaning inward like a slanted drunk, staying on his feet but just a notch away from falling forward. Trace the shadow a fence casts toppled inward on its meagre pension. Rub the sagging paling protecting children from the snarling dog-yard. Respect that fence refusing to be necessary, suggesting connection more than separation, a path across a vacant lot, ready to be worn.

Fences can tax the watcher, flirt with a passerby. They can undress the property they surround, shuck its mystery. They can annex and argue, advertise and administer. They can remark boom or bust, or they can be just fence, doing nothing but fencing, hanging between tracts of air like a stage curtain. Fences are merely fences, framed by what they cannot keep out, homesick as separation.

A fence is a plot, a ritual in the pattern of movement. A fence has a posture; it regards its own division sceptically, erect with watchful balance.

What is the conversation of a fence? A tensed body, the skeleton stretched past its outer digits. The dream of open land. We can drift against a fence in a blizzard, note its spillage and prevention.

There are gangster fences, adulterous, censoring. A fence may pretend to be solicitous, persuasive. A fence can wear its own handcuffs. A fence can be gangrenous, torpid.

Once there were no fences. Once there were no city blocks, no property. Cowboys took pride in cutting barbed wire and making campfires of the first fence-posts. Fear is the highest fence. All we can hope, in fencing the unfenceable, is to pattern our sidewalks and streets, recognize governance and taxes. And if once drifts of dust piled against the fences like snow, better to remember the hardy fence-line thorn that signs Alberta's springtime.

Meanwhile the sky threads toothpicks of telephone poles and electrical wires above, and although fences allocate and surround, they write geometrical poetry in this city of strange divisions.

SIGNS

Calgary's signs ride road and sidewalk, hoarding and wall, marquee and cipher. They are gesture and taboo, rune and incantation, casting a spell over this city even while they spell out our brand, our brash early morning autograph of black coffee and bitumen smiles, hands on the wheel, foot on the accelerator.

Signs cheerful as clear water trademark this Calgary. Come to me. Sell a dream. Buy a dream. Catch a check. Cash a cheque.

For Sale: one left-handed thumb, one exploded tire from an 18-wheeler. Corrective lenses, sedation dentistry.

Sign-painters have long vanished, returning just before Stampede to quick-draw cowboys and horses on plate-glass, painting the imaginary history that celebrates our long-lost ranch and its carnival.

Reasonably priced: shoes, beer, jeans, leather furniture, brisk winds.

Fresh squeezed: into those faded blue denims, those boots half a size too small, that tarnished belt buckle left over from last year.

Lotteries and Dreams: married in a hurry, quick, giddy-up, hope for lightning to strike and love to last.

Every sign incites a shadow, a historic muscle from the moment it appears, its message lyrical, connecting desire with its object. Find that significance, its goal a reminder, eye-catcher, cow-catcher, a coming together of attention and desire.

Exit: do not take this turn, do not escape, but arrive over and over. Wait for the end of entrance or for beginning to become middle.

Diesel: fuel waiting for the spark to ignite, internal combustion, exhaust.

Gas: payless plus discount, pay at the pump, full service, fill 'er up.

Signs of the physical world wait for no discount: snow heralds coming winter; sunset unveils coming night; the body offers up stigmata of expectation, symptom, cure, and prognosis. We'll trade, the sign says, what you want for what you have.

Tune-up: the steam locomotive, the right elbow, the window seat.

Powers of observation: the mason and Paskapoo sandstone; the mechanic and the car; the horse and the prairie, not a saddle in sight.

No Smoking: that's a given, a spare directive commonplace as the butt-littered ground in the lee of doorways, portals meant to imagine interchange. Beyond the entrance lives a smile that can turn a wall into a window, make plastic flowers bloom.

Swear: on a stack of coffee cups, on the sticky plastic cover of a menu, on the edge of a rickety table. Place your bets here.

Open: beyond business hours lurk days and months. Minutes record themselves hastily, take time seriously, but the hours, ah, they are luxurious with waiting, and the days come and go, talking of restless seasons that betray all expectations, summer in winter and winter in the spring, no way to prepare for snow or heat, the chinook blustering the moment when prairie meets mountain, and shushes the arctic air, softens it like warming butter.

All you can eat: of hope, of dust, of optimism, of disappointment. Ambrosia one day and nettles the next, those appetites driving this city's wax and wane. Rapid contractions a matter of course, as sharp as a sudden cough, economy's bubble and default. Here is no cycle but a swing, loose and creaking, mourning a rider.

A sign ceases to be a sign when you cannot read it. Then it becomes sibylline, oracular.

Suites: instrumental or orchestral, unified by key, like the repeated pattern of stacked apartments, flats in a collage, intermezzi connecting rooms, the city packaging its rentals, payment and yield in the pursuit of use.

Contract: to make smaller, excavate. Dig, scoop, unearth. The dig of disinter and exhume, and the industrious intent of spade and shovel, work waiting to shingle a roof or the side of a building.

Boarded up habitation, windows become hoardings that frame waiting, independent ideas lurched into hiding. Plywood nailed windows sign anticipation, the pause before metamorphosis, recreation out there waiting to happen, a new dream to splinter glass secrets.

Pawn: three spheres suspended from a bar, back to the house of Lombard. This old guitar. This necklace tarnished by recent romance. This saloon table wet with bottle rings. This pistol hot to the touch. These carpentry tools in a city made of concrete, woodworking now out of touch with itself. This clock radio, determined to strike fear into sleep. This ark that will ride the flood until a sprig of green appears again. This exit sign. This waltz, its silent glide, its gentle clench, two-beat and tender. Pawn your own shadow, your persistent insomnia, your hostage demands. Calgary's trademark, traded in. To locate stolen items, visit pawn shops. This loan, repayment of hope and expectation. Our arbitrary logic, that weakest of all chess pieces.

The essence of a sign is to convey information, to reach out and touch the eyes, to speak like a finger pointing, like a vibration under the skin, likely biopsy.

Second-hand. Collateral for what can never be outdated.

Vintage hand-painted signs yearn for the future that has bypassed them. They relic announcement, so carefully letraset onto once-prosperous brick walls, now flaking into thin air, nostalgic for the businesses they named, hieroglyphics weathered by wind.

Promises for sale: the ring on the finger, the parted curtains, the draped figure, the fervent light, a wink, a fever, tattoos and same day delivery.

Find the needle in the haystack. Avoid that melting snowdrift. Wait for the fresh gravesite, coming this week, on special. And always-hopeful faces selling quizzical ambition, belief in tomorrow's dream, or at least renewal.

For Sale: music and motion, the quick glare of a bare leg, an acre of fence, payday loans, bliss and perdition.

ROUGH

No time to smooth the edges, to polish outlines and buff up shoe leather. Calgary is a binge city, gulping this split second down before it evaporates. No patina of venerable time here, no legends backing up street names or stairways. We are the irregulars, roughed up and down, coarse as an old horse's mane, a ruffian shout. This boisterous, careless city, at its guttural ease.

In years to come we'll re-visit spaces orphaned by transition, try to track down that rickety veranda, that murderous mud room where we left our dust and impatience, our mismatched gloves and shabby hats.

New and used cohabit, auto parts dating gas and wash, angle parking determined to outlast winter's smothered light. Always portable, utilitarian, a moveable site picks itself up and migrates around the corner. Grease and gasoline, companions after all these years, still lurch along together, finishing one another's sentences and sleeping spooned in the middle of a saggy mattress.

There are names for us: difficult, turbulent, vulgar, still packed in the crates we were shipped in. But we cherish these guttural worksites, splinters in this city's private heart. Even while we bristle at our own depiction we stenograph a painted face, avert our eyes, and retreat shyly from this city's growing graveyard lush with stone and steel, handsome as hope. We refuse to quarantine the infectious, we ignore crumbling cement, curbs edging back quack grass and the headstrong prairie. We know our absent mythology and marble. We defend the nervous little strip mall trying too hard to manage, shoddy but determined.

Pull on the leather jacket with scuffed shoulders, cruise ragged roads that echo their gravel origins. Sit down at tables holding up the elbows that have worn them into patterns. No cloth-covered luxury, the shabby edges round toward replacement, polish the naugahyde of booths. Tables propose service, crumpled bills and a coffee spoon, drinks all around on slow afternoons thronged with beer glasses, bottles of light a slow leach of colour.

Celebrate the perfect disorder of alleys, rusty hinges behind the towers that cluster downtown Calgary like gold-capped teeth. There were acres here, holding their own against the sky, the sentinel poles standing in for people, like erect gophers. And the puzzled mosaic of cranes, ladders inching toward crossword grids. *Cranus eructus*, building sky out of sky, reaching across blue. No touch but to touch. Nothing but suggestion, the honeycombed buildings waiting to be filled, egg-cartons on end, their windows custom art in a repetition of space, dancing with refraction.

For here is a city climbing a ladder to heaven, exploring luminous air with erector-set resolve. Cranes do exactly that, crane extended necks to winch the honeycombed ambitions of not-yet imagined buildings. On the ground, the rubble that bedrocks those soaring structures coats itself with ash, beautiful debris. We perplex the sky with bolts and strips, girders and brackets; and behind the city's back, the river rolls by under a boa of mist.

Calgary is a wire-strung city, no fear of heights, just a smile for the ascent. Or a painted face to wear during Stampede, our annual jamboree, carnival in defiance of thunderheads or poor harvests, shrove and party saturnalia homage to our *carne*, carnage, *carnis*. Burlesque spurned inhibition, no shabby demise but a dancing soubrette and an invitation to remember the corner where we sat in the sun, hoping for heat.

And why not take pride in private parking, exuberant weeds? Why not extol the flat caps of the roofs holding down the city's historic insomnia? Somewhere rest local pools of disinclination, ferocious with quiet, a perpetual hush before the inevitable freeze. We expect snow to come stealthily, easing the black of lengthening night. Everything, when the snow skiffs, turns blue, the sky, the roads, the stream of cars on pilgrimage to tomorrow. Exits wait for those twilights of incipient blizzard, crystals preceding the elegance of winter and the light washed pale and liquid, strained by theatre.

To be honest, natural light is unnatural here, refuses to take its cues from reflection. It haloes cinematography, the drop-off distance from one point to another. This is hard light, cut-throat as a straight razor with a balance problem. Only a master barber can take this blade to the city's throat, exposed but not nervous, while the roads strop the buildings that hang between earth and yonder.

Rough it. Saddle up, brick down, open out, and while the green flash still lingers, resist what saddens the eyes and dance the tarantella, frenzied and yet stately, court cabaret, colloquial caricature, double the light quick steps.

As for money, let's invent it. Payroll cash deposit title loan sales, numbers blurred, a slip of paper folded into softness. Tattoos for lease and jokers for rent. Sold waits for the hour to broker settlement, to relax its sadness and declare a conclusion. After the rubble of industrial dirt, aggregate pebbles and dust. Rundle or sandstone rune where we were before we were here, this city's footsteps from the past, dinosaur tracks that we've forgotten how to read.

Rough is a dealer's felt, a coffee pot's grind, a tomato plant's leaves. Rough is what's past the edge of the postcard, the tempting cliff, the infraction of work, sweet exertion's fatigue, and rhubarb pushing through frost.

REQUIEM

There are a dozen cities where one might choose to grow old, their literary homecomings thick with temptation. Those are the places that seethe with pilgrims, where postcard racks adorn sidewalks and the same bells have rung for centuries, tours of significant sites available hourly. But those cities taste of their own indigestion, wield a language lethargic with habit. They are complacent; their bones crack when they shift.

What are our vices? A town with a taste for riddles and disguises, all of us rodeo clowns, waving to attract danger. We've no use for ornamental knowledge or extravagant devotion, do not inherit our houses or professions. We rise early in order to re-invent ourselves before breakfast. We finish the job we've contracted, the horizon we've arranged for, the sleep that will temper our impatience.

This city isn't gritty enough to be beautiful. No one believes us brave and confident. We're considered bland as a button, energetic but heedless, industrious enough, generous but intolerant. Quick to turn a collar and stride away, ripe with impatient justice. Yet, here is our destination and yearning: the greedy sprawl, the stubborn tenderness of the harsh light. We are modest folks who keep the secrets of this city. Even as they arrive, we discourage newcomers, those who move for their own consumption. No one comes here for pleasure, but for ambition, that philistine affection. And we're too kind to measure out the balance sheet of merit. Yet those who open their arms to the city's temper are seduced, fall in love between the CPR tracks stitching the corridor of downtown and the parabola of the Bow.

People expect that Calgary will forget them when they leave. Instead, they discover longing, the wisp of desire aching to return, the promise that it will be possible to close their eyes here against the glare of stolen time. We think that we are separate from this city. That we live here but do not live here, mere bystanders to its crazy spread, its rumoured consumption.

What is our rhythm? Clop-along or anguished guitars? Slow fiddle or furious drums? It is the cadence of the chinook, picking up in the night to remind us that this city was blown here by law and liquor and locomotion. That the rivers gleamed promise but the hills were tough to climb, and vice had to be concocted.

We are reticent as our own obscurity. Late at night, under a stalking moon, our history sings behind closed doors. Night infects our waiting. What is the archetype of Calgary?

A faded sign, a bloated sunset? A bleak facade that cannot shelter the wind? That wind our city wall, while the noisy bars serve as our cathedrals, worth a visit to say a quick novena, to mourn what's lost. Sleepless as the coming cold, always stealing up behind the short, high summer, the mauve line of the foothills kneeling at the horizon, far enough away to disappear our gaze. The power of Calgary is that the world does not know us, does not even want to, dismisses our gas stations and brusque roads, assumes we are forsaken, mangy, distempered.

We might petition ourselves to be braver, but this is a vulnerable city, shy, taciturn to a fault. We hesitate to speak, and when we do, cannot help but declare a series of truths. *Your radishes taste delicious. The train is late again. I want to tell you that I want to fall in love with you. Again. I have found your gloves. Be gentle with me.*

What are we missing? Maze-like alleys, street sweepers and feral dogs, a *zocalo*. We have instead cougars and coyotes and green stretches, inconvenient but determined. Wolf willow and sage still crouch in the draw of ravines. Drive up Crowchild in a convertible on a hot August night to be converted: to glimpse an embryo of what this city might become if we dare to enjoy it. No gates that proclaim entrance, just the arteries of roads, as sinuous as the fractures of the coulees that they follow. Garrets, eager for poets to sequester themselves, are scarce, as rare as beautiful girls waiting to dance. Only the signs of windows closed by curtains, reflections caught accidentally in a double wake.

We carry sorrows aplenty, are home to grieving widows, waifs and strays, migrants and expatriates. Calgary does not crush heartbreak, but cradles hope, gently, in both hands. We are a city too small for loitering, too big for privacy, too hesitant for balance, and yet too tenacious to be dismissed. Neither sexy nor indifferent, but in our own absent way attentive, and if restless, willing to wait. We want comfortable boots, a good warm scarf, and most of all, a kindly ghost, one who walks before dawn, one who lurks in glass distortions, liquid sand holding this city up to the light.

I picture a future when I'll return to this elusive season, this city in its shining. That hour between day and twilight, just before the street lamps blink, and when the shadows of the Rockies dwindle, hovering out there in a mirage that denies these sidewalks, these blurred and deceptive roads. Pink paint flakes around a window, tough apples fall, and overall, the slow gold of fading light as thick as batter spills over the curbs and the puddles left by receding sudden storms.

If the skies take to hiding we will recreate them, flashbulbs of intensity. And as for passions, what rouses the eye searching the horizon? A quick and restless wind? What sets us wandering past signs and into sun-drenched hideouts where we begin to talk about the way we were, traces of a present already slipped away?

So requiem it is. Calgary is where I will take my human bows, where I will totter on a crosswalk and hope for the kindness of strangers.

In this place.

CALGARY STAMPEDE – 2007

GAS PLUS

DIESEL

DISCOUNT
GAS
PRICES
CHECK IT OUT

AUTO
PROPANE
42.9
CENTS/LITRE

MOVING?

U-HAUL

6813 OGDEN ROAD SE – 2009

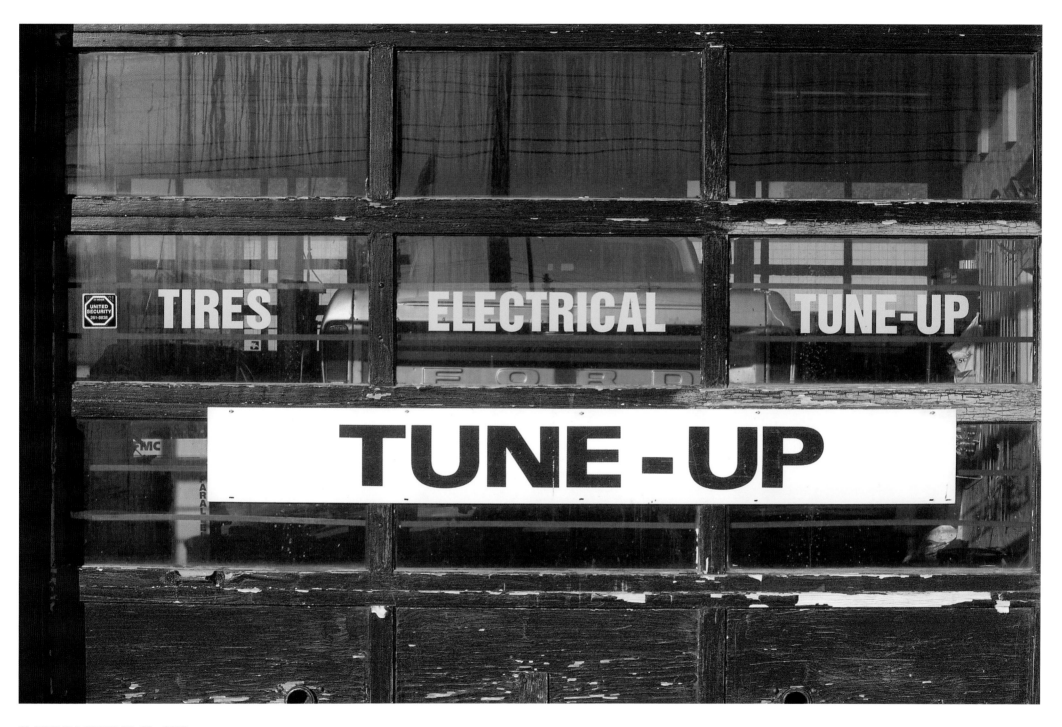

69 AVENUE & OGDEN RD. SE – 2007

2006 SPILLER ROAD – 2011

DOWNTOWN CALGARY – 2007

CENTRE STREET & 17 AVENUE SW – 2007

NEAR 36 AVENUE & 2 STREET NE – 2010

5216 6 STREET NE – 2007

2704 52 STREET SE – 2009

68 AVENUE & OGDEN ROAD SE – 2006

35 STREET & 17 AVENUE SE – 2005

4 SEAS RESTAURANT, 17 AVENUE SE – 2009

4 SEAS RESTAURANT, 17 AVENUE SE – 2009

MARLA CROWTHER, 4 SEAS RESTAURANT, 17 AVENUE SE – 2009

24 STREET & OGDEN ROAD SE – 2007

1223A 9 AVENUE SE (REAR) – 2011

15A STREET & OGDEN ROAD SE – 2009

CHINATOWN – 2010

CHINATOWN – 2010

CHINATOWN – 2010

CHINATOWN – 2010

工藝精品　日用百貨

保健藥材

中國食品

FOR LEASE

安樂餐

CHINATOWN – 2010

CHINATOWN – 2010

BARRY RILEY, HOLIDAY MOTEL, 4550 16 AVENUE NW – 2008

534 12 AVENUE SE – 2007

1100 BLOCK 42 STREET SE – 2007

CENTENNIAL LEGION – 2007

OGDEN LEGION – 2007

TODD DAVIES, OGDEN LEGION – 2007

LEGION NUMBER 1 – 2007

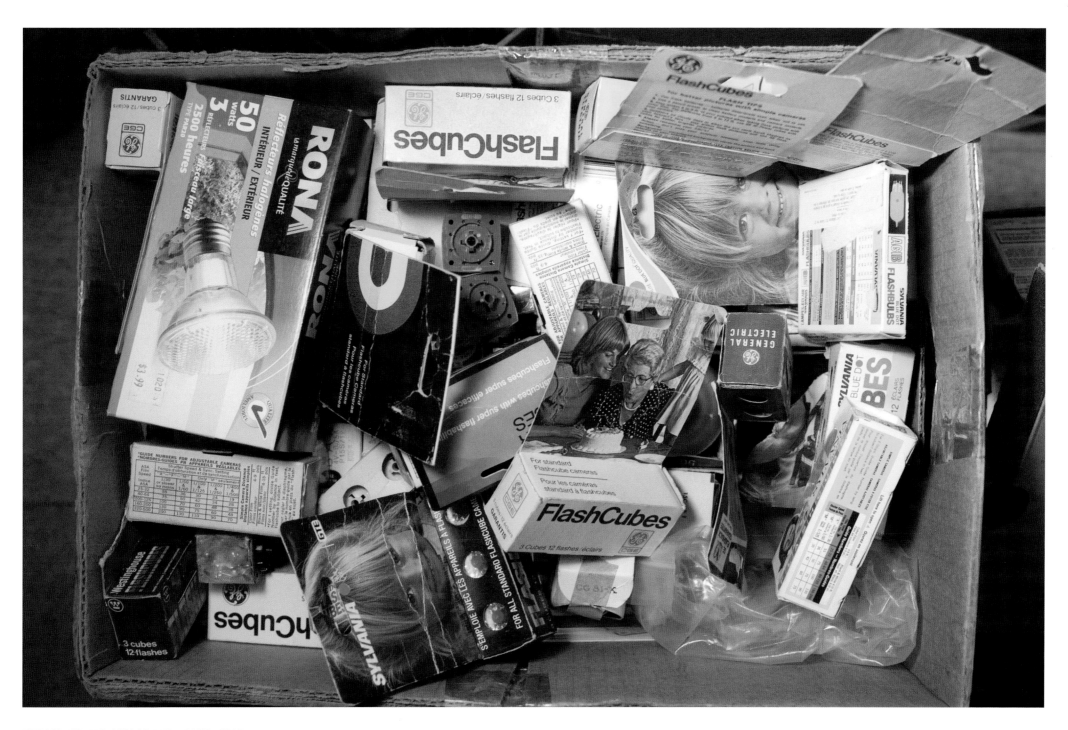

VINTAGE VISUALS, 1020 16 AVENUE NW – 2006

3233 17 AVENUE SE – 2009

CARTWORLD, 5202 1 STREET SW – 2008

3500 BLOCK 17 AVENUE SE – 2006

CENTRE STREET – 2006

3500 BLOCK 17 AVENUE SE – 2007

2010 11 STREET SE (REAR) – 2007

COYOTES, NEAR 11 AVENUE & OLYMPIA WAY SE – 2007

121 7 AVENUE SW (REAR) – 2009

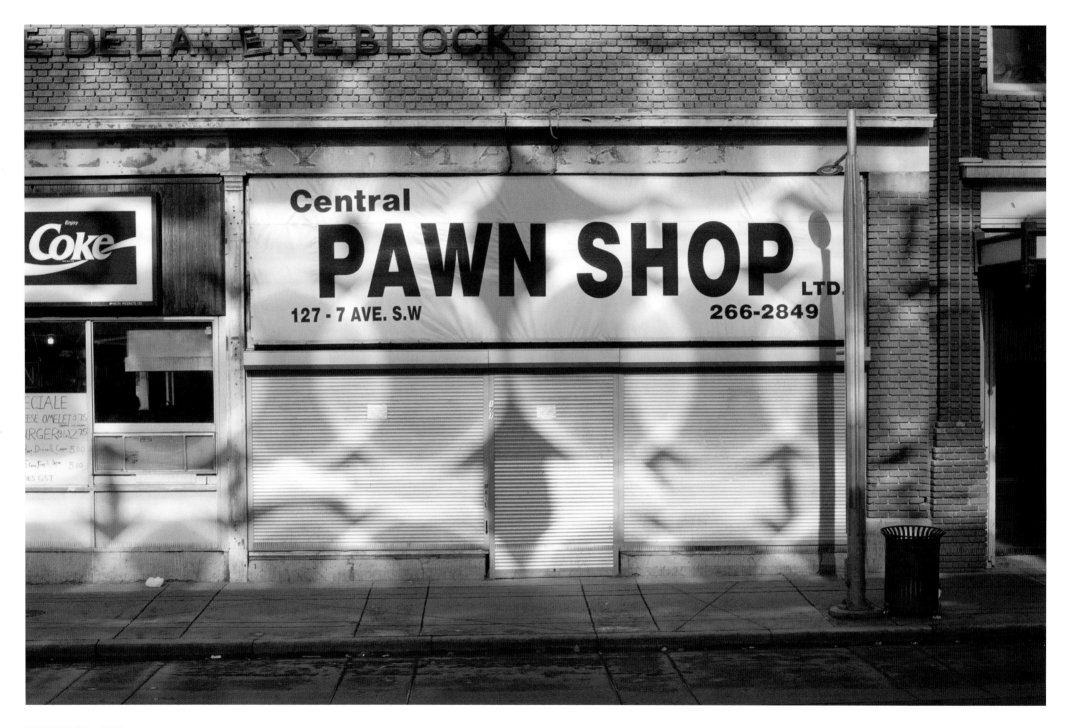

7 AVENUE SW – 2008

7 AVENUE SW – 2007

2700 BLOCK, 16 STREET SE – 2006

ACE SALVAGE, 280 OGDEN ROAD SE – 2009

120 16 AVENUE NE – 2011

1229 - 1231 MACLEOD TRAIL SW – 2009

3609 17 AVENUE SE – 2008

3400 BLOCK, 17 AVENUE SE – 2006

222 17 AVENUE SW – 2007

1212 45 AVENUE NE – 2010

16 AVENUE & 12 STREET NW – 2007

THE UPTOWN THEATRE, 610 8 AVENUE SW – 2008

4 STREET NEAR 10 AVENUE SW – 2007

FRANK SCHROEDER , 9 AVENUE SE – 2006

LANCE HUGHES , ST LOUIS HOTEL – 2006

HUDSON'S BAY WINDOW, DOWNTOWN – 2005

GARTER GIRLS – 2010

GARTER GIRLS – 2010

GARTER GIRLS – 2010

GARTER GIRLS – 2010

BEERLAND, CECIL HOTEL – 2009

ROLLERLAND, 42 STREET & 8 AVENUE SE – 2007

4815 17 AVENUE SE (REAR) – 2009

BEERLAND & DROP IN CENTRE – 2009

NEAR 52 STREET & 20 AVENUE SE – 2009

VICTORIA PARK SE – 2007

ACKNOWLEDGEMENTS

I am very grateful to Frontenac House for making the creation of this book so much fun, to Aritha van Herk for her sparkling and insightful words and to Neil Petrunia for his craftsmanship and good taste in the realization of *In This Place*.

- George Webber

Thank you to Frontenac House, to George Webber for the moody pictures, to the Glenbow Museum and Archives, the Calgary Public Library, and my students at the University of Calgary. You have helped me to plumb the heart of this city.

Thanks as well to the University of Alberta Press for permission to quote from Robert Kroetsch's *The Snowbird Poems*.

- Aritha van Herk